FAST!
SPEEDBOATS

... and other fast machines in the water

QEB Publishing

IAN GRAHAM

The words in **bold** are explained in the Glossary on page 30.

Front cover: A powerboat racer
skims across the top of the waves
(see page 20).

Project Editor: Angela Royston
Designer: Andrew Crowson
Picture Researcher: Maria Joannou

Published in the United States by
QEB Publishing, Inc.
3 Wrigley, Suite A
Irvine, CA 92618

www.qed-publishing.co.uk

Library of Congress Cataloging-in-Publication Data

Graham, Ian, 1953-
  Speedboats / Ian Graham.
    p. cm. -- (Fast!)
  Includes bibliographical references and index.
  ISBN 978-1-59566-929-2 (library binding : alk. paper)
  1. Motorboats--Juvenile literature. 2. Motorboat racing--
Juvenile literature. I. Title.
  GV835.G73 2011
  797.1'4--dc22

                        2010006063

Printed in China

Picture credits

Alamy Images Mary Evans Picture Library 4–5, Justin
Prenton 5t, Trinity Mirror/Mirrorpix 18t, 24t, Danita
Delimont 22–23; **American Challenge, Inc** 29b; **Corbis**
Neil Rabinowitz 23t, Stringer 7tl, Patrick Durand 14;
Department of Defense 7b; **Florida Atlantic University**
7tr; **Getty Images** China Photos/Stringer FC, Science
& Society Picture Library 8b, Hulton Archive/Stringer
9c, Kos Picture Source 12, Cate Gillon 13t, AFP/Marcel
Mochet 13b, 16–17, AFP/Gerard Julien 16b, Hulton
Archive/Central Press/Stringer 18–19, AFP/Stringer 20t,
AFP/Cris Bouroncle 21t, 21c; **INCAT** Trevor Kidd 15t,
Fjord Line 15c; **Photolibrary** National Motor Museum
24–25, 25tl, 25tr; **Press Association Images** Nigel
Bennetts/PA Archive 15b, Jim Bryant/AP 23c; **QWSR
Ltd** 29t, 29c; **Rex Features** 20-21, Daily Mail 8–9, Phil
Rees 13c, Sipa Press 17r, Newspix 26t, 28; **SailRocket**
10–11, 11t, 11bl, 11br; **Shutterstock** Rodolfo Arpia 9b,
Joe Stone BC; **Topham Picturepoint** 19t, 19c, UPP
26–27, 27t; **U.S. Navy** 6; **Wikimedia Commons** Alfred
John West 5b

Contents

Note: The boats appear in order of speed, from the slowest to the fastest.

Fastest in the water

The first speed records on water were set by boats with steam engines. Boats have been getting faster ever since.

Turbinia's long slender hull sliced through the water easily.

Turbinia

In 1894, the fastest boat in the world was called *Turbinia*. It was the first boat with a **steam turbine engine**. The spinning turbine turned the boat's **propeller**. *Turbinia* impressed Britain's Royal Navy so much that they decided to power all new warships with steam turbine engines.

Jet-powered hydroplanes are the fastest boats.

Speeding up

In the 1920s, racing boats set faster and faster records. Today, there are **jet-powered** boats and boats that fly above the water! The fastest boats are **hydroplanes** that skim the waves at faster speeds than a jet airliner! The power of a boat's engine is measured in **horsepower.**

FACTFILE

Turbinia

- Length: 103.7 feet (31.6 meters)
- Weight: 45 tons
- Engine: Steam turbine
- Power: 2,000 horsepower
- Top speed: 39 miles per hour (63 kilometers per hour)
- Crew: Unknown

HOW FAST?

Turbinia moved more than twice as fast as a modern oil tanker.

Under the Waves

Submarines can go faster under the water than on top of it. Waves on the surface slow them down. When they dive, they pick up speed because the water flows around them more smoothly.

Fast subs

The first of the fast modern submarines was the U.S. Navy's *Albacore*. Its **hull** was shaped like a teardrop so that it slipped through the water very easily. This submarine had a top speed of 38 miles per hour (61 kilometers per hour) underwater. Russian Akula class submarines are even faster.

The USS *Albacore* was launched in 1953.

Talon-1 is a human-powered submarine propelled by a diver inside it.

Muscle power

Races are held every year to find the fastest human-powered submarine. One or two divers inside each submarine pedal to turn the propeller! The 2009 International Submarine Races were won by *Talon-1* at a speed of 7.2 miles per hour (11.6 kilometers per hour)—three or four times faster than walking speed.

Russian Akula class submarines are very fast underwater and also very quiet.

Fastest liner

The Blue Riband is an honor given to the fastest passenger liner to cross the Atlantic Ocean in regular passenger service.

Super Sirius

The Blue Riband has been held by 23 British ships, five German, three American, one Italian, and one French. The first holder of the Blue Riband was a British paddle steamer called *Sirius* in 1838. Its steam engine turned a big paddle wheel on each side of the ship. At that time a **transatlantic** voyage took up to 40 days, but *Sirius* made the crossing in just 18 days.

Sirius had to burn all of its fuel supply of coal and also some furniture to finish its Atlantic crossing.

SS *United States* was launched in 1952 and immediately became the fastest transatlantic liner.

The United States

The last of the great passenger liners to hold the Blue Riband was the SS *United States*. It was nearly five times longer than *Sirius* and 24 times heavier, but it was much faster. In 1952, it crossed the ocean in only three and a half days—more than four times faster than *Sirius*.

FACTFILE

SS *United States*

- Length: 991 feet (302 meters)
- Weight: 43,000 tons
- Engine: Four steam turbines
- Power: 248,000 horsepower
- Top speed: 43 miles per hour (70 kilometers per hour)
- Crew: 900

HOW FAST?

SS *United States* crossed the Atlantic Ocean as fast as a racing cyclist.

The British liner RMS *Queen Mary* held the Blue Riband for the fastest Atlantic crossing from 1938 until 1952.

Super skimmer

A yacht called *SailRocket* is one of the most extreme sailing boats ever built, and one of the fastest.

Beam boat

This strange-looking yacht has a sail at one end of a long beam and a **cockpit** at the other end. The pilot sits in the cockpit and pushes pedals to control the sail and **rudders**.

SailRocket's sail is held at exactly the right angle to give the fastest speed.

Flying sail

SailRocket's sail stands on a **float**. As the boat speeds up, the float lifts out of the water. The sail flies along, and the cockpit skims across the surface of the water. At top speed, the rudders lift out of the water to make the boat go even faster. On December 4, 2008, its speed was measured at a record-breaking 54.4 miles per hour (87.6 kilometers per hour).

The sail is made of stiff material so that it stays in the perfect shape.

The pilot's helmet is shaped like this to help him cut through the wind.

FACTFILE

SailRocket

- Length: 36 feet (11 meters)
- Weight: 310 pounds (140 kilograms)
- Engine: None
- Power: Wind power
- Top speed: 54.4 miles per hour (87.6 kilometers per hour)
- Crew: 1

HOW FAST?

At top speed, *SailRocket* travels the same length as a soccer field in just 4 seconds.

Round the World

When the first voyages around the world were made in the 16th century, they took about three years. Since then, sailors have been going around the world faster and faster.

Going solo

In 2005, French yachtsman Bruno Peyron set a round-the-world record of 50 days. His yacht, *Orange II*, had a crew of 13. In 2007, another French yachtsman, Francis Joyon, broke the record for sailing around the world on his own. He made the solo voyage in his yacht *IDEC II* in 57 days.

The record-breaking yacht *Orange II* is a catamaran—it has two hulls.

Earthrace was powered by two diesel engines.

Earthrace

In 2008, a powerboat called *Earthrace* circled the world in 61 days. This was a record time for powerboats. *Earthrace* is a trimaran—it has three hulls. Two small hulls keep the bigger middle hull steady in the water.

FACTFILE

Earthrace

- Length: 79 feet (24 meters)
- Weight: 26 tons with full fuel tanks
- Engine: Two diesel engines
- Power: 540 horsepower
- Top speed: 54.9 miles per hour (88.3 kilometers per hour)
- Crew: 4

HOW FAST?

Earthrace goes through the water faster than the fastest shark.

IDEC II was designed to be sailed very fast by only one person.

Crossing the Atlantic

The Hales Trophy is awarded to any kind of passenger ship that makes the fastest crossing of the Atlantic Ocean. A ship can win the trophy even if it does not normally cross the Atlantic.

Water jets

In 1990, an ocean-going passenger ship called *Hoverspeed Great Britain* crossed the ocean in a record time of 3 days, 7 hours, 54 minutes. It was powered by waterjet engines. They suck in seawater and pump it out behind the ship at high speed.

Hoverspeed Great Britain's slim hulls slice easily through the waves.

Catalonia was later renamed *Express*. It carries 225 cars and 877 passengers.

Cat Link V

In 1998, a bigger passenger ship called *Catalonia* broke the transatlantic record, but the new record stood for only six weeks. It was broken by *Cat Link V*, the first commercial passenger vessel to cross the Atlantic Ocean in less than three days. During the record-breaking crossing, it stopped to help search for a missing plane, but still made the crossing in 2 days 20 hours!

FACTFILE

Cat Link V

- Length: 299 feet (91 meters)
- Weight: 510 tons
- Engine: Four marine diesel engines
- Power: 34,000 horsepower
- Top speed: 55 miles per hour (89 kilometers per hour)
- Crew: Unknown

HOW FAST?

Cat Link V is about 1.5 times faster than a naval destroyer.

Cat Link V was renamed *Fjord Cat*. It is the world's fastest passenger vessel.

Flying yacht

The fastest sailing boat in the world flies above the water! Flying over the waves instead of pushing through them lets a boat go faster.

Underwater wings

When a yacht called *Hydroptère* is sitting still in the water, it looks like a normal sailing boat. But hidden below it are underwater wings called foils. They work like aircraft wings. As the yacht speeds up, the foils "fly" through the water. They slowly raise the boat higher and higher, until its whole hull is out of the water.

Hydroptère takes off as it picks up speed and its underwater foils start to work.

On December 21, 2008, *Hydroptère* briefly reached a speed of 70 miles per hour (112 kilometers per hour) before overturning in strong wind.

Finding materials

When boat-builders dreamt up *Hydroptère* in the mid-1970s, they had no materials strong enough and light enough to build it. By 1994, however, they were able to build *Hydroptère* using **carbon fiber** and **titanium**. On September 4, 2009, its speed was measured at 59 miles per hour (95.1 kilometers per hour), making it the fastest yacht in the world.

FACTFILE

Hydroptère

- Length: 58 feet (18 meters)
- Weight: 6.5 tons
- Engine: None
- Power: Wind power
- Top speed: 59 miles per hour (95.1 kilometers per hour)
- Crew: 9

HOW FAST?

Although it is powered only by the wind, *Hydroptère* goes twice as fast as RMS *Titanic* could.

Bluebirds

After breaking the land speed record for the last time in 1935, British racing driver Malcolm Campbell turned his attention to the world water speed record.

Malcolm Campbell wore little protective clothing—just a pair of goggles and a life jacket.

Bluebird K3

Bluebird K3 was Campbell's first record-breaking boat. This type of boat is called a hydroplane. It goes fast by skimming across the water's surface. *Bluebird K3* was powered by an aircraft engine. On September 1, 1937, Campbell set a water speed record of 126 miles per hour (203 kilometers per hour) on Lake Maggiore in Switzerland. He broke his own record twice more.

Campbell sits in the cockpit in front of *Bluebird K3*'s huge engine.

Bluebird K4

To go even faster, Campbell had a new boat built. *Bluebird K4* used the same engine as *K3*, but the boat was a different shape. On August 19, 1939, Campbell set his last and fastest water speed record of 142 miles per hour (228 kilometers per hour) on an English lake called Coniston Water.

Campbell set a new speed record in *Bluebird K3* on Lake Hallwyl in Switzerland, in 1938.

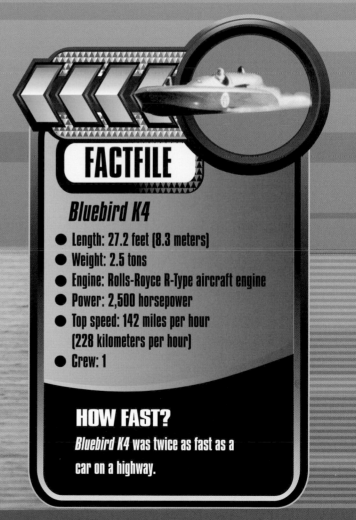

FACTFILE

Bluebird K4

- Length: 27.2 feet (8.3 meters)
- Weight: 2.5 tons
- Engine: Rolls-Royce R-Type aircraft engine
- Power: 2,500 horsepower
- Top speed: 142 miles per hour (228 kilometers per hour)
- Crew: 1

HOW FAST?

Bluebird K4 was twice as fast as a car on a highway.

Powerboat racers

Big powerboats race each other across the sea. Today's powerboats are faster than Malcolm Campbell's Bluebirds.

Two hulls

The fastest sea-going racers are Class 1 Powerboats. These racing boats have two hulls, one beside the other. Boats with two hulls are called catamarans. There is an engine in the tail end of each hull. Each boat has a crew of two. The crew wear **fireproof** overalls and helmets, like motor-racing drivers.

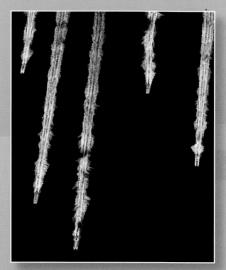

Class 1 powerboats race through the water, leaving foaming trails behind them.

A Class 1 powerboat is up to 46 feet (14 meters) long and weighs 5 tons.

Ocean-going racers are ten times more powerful than a family car.

Faster and faster

In the 1960s, powerboats could win a race with a speed of 30 miles per hour (50 kilometers per hour). In the 1980s, they were reaching speeds of more than 100 miles per hour (160 kilometers per hour). Now, a winning boat often speeds across the water at more than 125 miles per hour (200 kilometers per hour).

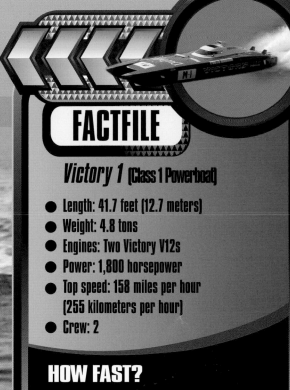

FACTFILE

Victory 1 (Class 1 Powerboat)

● Length: 41.7 feet (12.7 meters)
● Weight: 4.8 tons
● Engines: Two Victory V12s
● Power: 1,800 horsepower
● Top speed: 158 miles per hour (255 kilometers per hour)
● Crew: 2

HOW FAST?

At top speed, a Class 1 Powerboat could do a 90-minute car ferry journey in only 10 minutes.

Propeller boats

The last boat with a propeller to break the world water speed record was called *Slo-Mo-Shun IV*, but it wasn't a slow-motion boat.

Smashing records

On June 26, 1950, *Slo-Mo-Shun IV* smashed the water speed record with a speed of 160 miles per hour (258 kilometers per hour). Two years later, it raised the record to 178 miles per hour (287 kilometres per hour). After *Slo-Mo-Shun IV*, jet-powered boats took over as the world's fastest boats, so a separate record was set up for boats with propellers. In 2000, a propeller-driven boat called *Miss Freei* set a record of 205 miles per hour (330 kilometers per hour).

In 2000, *Miss Freei* broke a speed record that had stood for 38 years.

Miss Budweiser's cockpit cover is from an F-16 fighter plane.

Miss Budweiser

In 2004, *Miss Budweiser* pushed the record for propeller-driven boats up to 220 miles per hour (354 kilometers per hour). *Miss Budweiser* is powered by a helicopter engine. The engine spins the propeller 10,000 times a minute.

FACTFILE

Miss Budweiser

- Length: 29.9 feet (9.1 meters)
- Weight: 2.5 tons
- Engine: Lycoming turbine
- Power: 2,650 horsepower
- Top speed: 220 miles per hour (354 kilometers per hour)
- Crew: 1

HOW FAST?

Miss Budweiser can move as fast as a Formula 1 racing car.

The last Bluebird

Donald Campbell, the son of Malcolm Campbell (see page 18), built a new jet-powered boat to break the world water speed record.

Donald Campbell takes a break before his final record attempt in 1967.

Twice as fast

Donald Campbell's boat was called *Bluebird K7*. Between 1955 and 1964, he broke the water speed record seven times—more than anyone else. He raised the record to 276 miles per hour (444 kilometers per hour), nearly double his father's last record.

Donald Campbell's *Bluebird K7* jet-boat was the first to go faster than 185 miles per hour (300 kilometers per hour).

FACTFILE

Bluebird K7

- Length: 26 feet (8 meters)
- Weight: 2.5 tons
- Engine: Vickers "Beryl" jet engine
- Power: 3,200 horsepower
- Top speed: 276 miles per hour (444 kilometers per hour)
- Crew: 1

HOW FAST?

Bluebird K7 crossed the water faster than a Ferrari supercar goes on land.

The final challenge

On January 4, 1967, Bluebird K7 hurtled across Coniston Water at 296 miles per hour (477 kilometers per hour). To set a new record, the boat had to turn around and come back. Campbell was supposed to stop for fuel, but he didn't.

He started back down the lake. At top speed, the boat hit ripples in the water caused by the first run. The ripples raised Bluebird's nose and it took off. It flipped over and crashed into the water. Campbell died instantly.

Spirit of Australia

On October 8, 1978, Australian powerboat racer Ken Warby broke the world water speed record with a jet-boat he built in his backyard in Sydney.

Ken Warby gets ready to begin testing his boat *Spirit of Australia*.

A tale of a tail

When Warby tested a model of his boat, he discovered that it would take off if it went faster than 250 miles per hour (400 kilometers per hour)! He changed the design, and added a tail from a plane. These changes stopped the boat from taking off. Warby broke the water speed record—and lived to tell the tale!

Spirit of Australia

- Length: 26.9 feet (8.2 meters)
- Weight: Unknown
- Engine: Westinghouse J34 jet engine
- Power: 6,000 horsepower
- Top speed: 318 miles per hour (511 kilometers per hour)
- Crew: Ken Warby

HOW FAST?

Spirit of Australia sped across the water at more than half the speed of a jet airliner.

Spirit of Australia

Warby called his boat *Spirit of Australia*. In 1977, he set a new record speed of 288 miles per hour (464 kilometers per hour) at Blowering Dam in New South Wales, Australia. He thought *Spirit of Australia* could go even faster. He went back to Blowering Dam the following year and raised his own record to 318 miles per hour (511 kilometers per hour).

Warby sets his first world water speed record in 1977.

Future records

By 2010, Ken Warby's water speed record had stood unbroken for nearly 32 years. Two boats being designed now may challenge Warby's record one day.

Aussie Spirit

In the late 1990s, Ken Warby built a new boat called *Aussie Spirit* to try to break his own record. Then in 2007, at the age of 68, Warby decided to retire. Until someone else goes faster, he will be the fastest person ever on water.

Ken Warby's new boat, *Aussie Spirit*, was completed in 1999.

Quicksilver will be powered by a 10,000 horsepower jet engine.

Challengers

A British boat called *Quicksilver* could become the most powerful boat to try to break the world water speed record. Another boat, called the *American Challenge*, is being built in the United States. Both boats would be made of the latest materials used for planes and spacecraft.

FACTFILE

Quicksilver

Length: 38.7 feet (11.8 meters)
Weight: 3.5 tons
Engine: Rolls-Royce Spey jet engine
Power: 10,000 horsepower
Top speed: 330 miles per hour
(530 kilometers per hour)
Crew: 1

HOW FAST?

At top speed, *Quicksilver* could cross the Atlantic Ocean in 15 hours, a journey that takes six days by passenger liner.

American Challenge will be powered by two jet engines.

Glossary

carbon fiber A very strong, lightweight material made from plastic strengthened by strands of carbon.

cockpit The part of a boat, plane, or car where the driver or pilot and other crew members sit.

fireproof Able to resist fire. Fireproof clothing protects the person wearing it, because it does not burn.

float A hollow, watertight part of a boat that floats on water.

horsepower A measurement of the power of a machine such as a boat.

hull The main part of a boat or ship that sits in the water.

hydroplane A very fast speedboat that sits on top of the water instead of pushing through it like an ordinary boat.

jet-powered Pushed along by a jet engine.

propeller A device with angled blades that spins and pushes a boat along.

rudders Flat sheets or panels that hang down behind boats and are turned to steer them.

steam turbine engine A type of ship's engine that works by the power of steam produced by boiling water. A jet of steam makes a device called a turbine spin, which turns the ship's propeller.

titanium A strong, lightweight metal.

transatlantic Across the Atlantic Ocean.

turbine A drum with blades all around it. When a liquid or gas, such as a jet of steam, hits the blades, the drum spins. A turbine is part of a turbine engine.

Notes for parents and teachers

Shape and size

Look through the pictures in the book and talk about why the boats and ships are different shapes and sizes. Think about other vessels that are not included in this book, such as fishing boats and rowing boats, and talk about how they compare to the boats in this book.

Design

The fastest record-breaking boats are specially designed to go very fast. Think about how other types of boat are designed for different purposes. For example, motor cruisers and luxury yachts are comfortable, with space for passengers and bags. Cargo boats have big spaces inside, called holds, for carrying cargo.

Speed

Boats set speed records on closed courses specially set up for record-breaking, or far out at sea. Talk about why speed records are set in places where there are no other boats or swimmers in the water. Driving a boat very fast is dangerous. Talk about how the drivers of very fast boats try to stay safe by wearing a seatbelt, a helmet, and fireproof clothes.

Hulls

Most boats have one hull, but fast boats often have two or even three hulls. Think about why two or three hulls might be better than one. Why do fast boats have long, thin hulls, but some other boats have short, fat hulls?

Controls

Discuss the ways in which a driver controls a boat—a wheel to steer the boat and an accelerator pedal or thrust lever to go faster.

Drawing

Ask children to draw their own record-breaking boat. What would it look like? What shape would it be? What would it be made of? What sort of engine would it have? Where would it go to set its speed records? How fast do they think it would go?

Index